I0756247

FINISHING LINE PRESS
www.finishinglinepress.com

Waning into Winter

poems by

Martha Sherick Shen

Finishing Line Press
Georgetown, Kentucky

Waning into Winter

My life
At backward glance
Now
without buds or leaves
Waning into Winter
Learning to
Breathe through my Roots like the trees.

ISBN 979-8-89990-398-4 First Edition

ACKNOWLEDGMENTS

A Poet's Hymn first appeared in *Flying Island Journal* in April, 2024. This was the author's first published poem.

Hollywood Juniper first appeared in *Synkroniciti* in August, 2024. This was the author's second published poem and it was nominated for Best of the Net.

Publisher: Leah Huete de Maines
Editor: Christen Kincaid
Cover Art: Elanni Jade Sherick
Author Photo: Shen Family Photo
Cover Design: Elizabeth Maines McCleavy

Order online: www.finishinglinepress.com
also available on amazon.com

Author inquiries and mail orders:
Finishing Line Press
PO Box 1626
Georgetown, Kentucky 40324
USA

Contents

Dedicated to Sheldon Shen

With special gratitude to
Tina Denetclaw
For her unwavering faith, help and encouragement.
And deep thankfulness for my daughters:
Abra Nichol
And Elanni Jade Sherick
Without them, none of these poems would have been written.

O-zone

Words have become
a Single Vowel

no longer a Noun constrained by
Consonants
They are an Emotion
broader than a Verb
more pervasive than the
Wind
carried into Eternity…
they are
the Whisper of Dawn
a single
"O"

Do you feel how the Trees
are breathing you
into Life?
with a voracity
only rivaled by the Mosses
that Jumped the Land Barrier
and started the whole process in the first place
Breathing Us

Into
Existence.

Can you constrain
such a Thought?

The tree leaves osculate the heavens
as the stars oscillate in my mind
I breathe in their Life
and breathe out my single
"O"
into this Liminal Space

whose panoramic view
challenges my limited peripheral vision

while my Soul
  Unconstrained
      is a Single "O"
          on the Wind....

The "O" is symbolic for two things 1) the myriads of emotions connected to the exclamation "OH!" (such as delight/awe, empathy/sympathy understanding, questionings, anger/disgust etc.). It is also the scientific symbol for Oxygen. The world of science thinks that moss is the link between plant life on land and the ocean (it might have been algae that adapted to land). We did not have the stratospheric ozone layer to protect us before that... the plants put oxygen into the atmosphere...or we could never have survived. Moss always causes an exclamation of "O! how amazing!" And at the same time, I am breathing in the oxygen for my lungs!

In Awe of the Trees

I stand
in Awe of the Trees.

the mighty Catalpa
stretches to the Sky
she delves down firmly
drinking In the Earth.
Her ancient strength defies the forces
that seek to cause her demise
and she blossoms
clothed from head to toe
in an Alabaster vestige
she glows
radiant in the Breath of Eternity.

I behold the American Elm whose
tenacity overflows the
concrete of Civilization and carves her beauty into her bark.

I wonder,
is the texture of
My Being
evident in the Bark of my Experience,
in the complexion of my character?
Are my wandering branches draped in the
cortex of contemplation,
fruiting leaves
to Capture the Sun…?
Do my roots grow down deep to feed from the soil?

I see The Sycamore
White Ghost of Immortality
whose silhouette takes my breath away
She is most beautiful in the winter
divest of leaves
dancing in the early morning Light!

The Red bud
diminutive in stature
in Spring bursts a radiant magenta lace
Heavenly dressed
she proclaims her message
in heart shaped leaves
and twisted Grace.
Her glorious Presence resounds
a musical reprise

as I catch my breath
within me lies

a Holy Silence

i stand in Awe
an Attentive
Reverent guest.

I bow my head in praise
to the Living Lasting
Testament of the Trees
as the reticulation of their boughs beckon the Stars
and their halcyon headdresses, a haven for birdsong,
harmonize with the hymn in my heart.

the Trees converse with the Wind in wordless
Wisdom
Speaking of Life's mystery
surging through their xylem
they grow upward outward downward
inward
a synergy of Worth.

In Testament to the Trees

I reclaim my own birth.

Trusting the Process of the Struggle

The Hawthorn Tree
bright red berries succulent clusters
devoured by the Cedar Waxwing's arduous journey.
The seed
processed through their ravenous need
is cast aside
into the whims of the wind
the refuse of their pilgrimage plummets
…miles away into the humus of life.
buried in debris
the Radicle
delves down
to draw from the rich resources of organic matter.

a Radical Thought:
to trust the Process of the Struggle
in the depths of digestion,
in the dark of the Earth
so a tender stem can reach blindly for the light
in New Ground
with green fingers feeling their way
ready to burst
as Earth Bound it meets the Sky…
****
The Cottonwood
trusts the wind with its cottony cargo.
It stands ominous in pervasive grandeur
a massive testament to the Dark Process in
tandem with Light.

Its leaves are a camouflage for a caterpillar to consume
until she too spins tree-cotton spewed from
her depths

her solitary sarcophagus spun
she awaits Resurrection:
the Cecropia Moth

Mammoth among Moths
Struggles   Exhausted   tearing out of the dark recesses

too   tired   to fly
crumpled and helpless against predators

until the dark experience dries and she pumps Life into her
Wings

and then

the Night Sky is hers.
—so am i

Ulmus Americana

This tree I pass
everyday meandering:

Science put a name to it: Ulmus Americana,
The American Elm
but
IT claims neither a country or a name.

it is Majestic
deeply furrowed bark,
gnarled branches holding the Sky
Up
over the years of its sustained Life.

I ask:

is the texture
of My Being evident in
the bark of My existence, in the
complexion of my character? Are
my wondering branches draped in the cortex of
contemplation
fruiting leaves to capture the Sun?

what do I hold up?
what do I
sustain?

…how beautifully this tree lives and grows and
Dances in the early morning light.

let this Tree teach me how to Live
let this Tree
teach me how to Be.

Bark Exfoliation of the Sycamore Tree

the sycamore
dances in the winter
divest of leaves
Stark White Naked against
the thick black burly oaks and the night sky.
it sings in the wind
and sways
to the jubilant rhythm of the earth.

i
laugh
in amazement.

they say it grows so fast it
sheds its skin
like a snake
leaving only the white underbelly
visible.

but,
i know its secret

it simply likes to
dance
unhindered
free
in exaltation
in celebration
after populating the earth with a million
downy seeds.

then
in the spring, sedate
demure
it clothes itself with great huge leaves
hiding its ostentatious form
it gathers energy into festive seed balls

ornaments of worth
i squish into downy fluff
and smile
waiting
for the dance
to begin.

The Geography of Light

The Geography of Light!
comprised of Stardust and Explosions
creates unfathomable oceans
whose dark murky depths inhabit white fish

and grow Sun-glistened light-waves
forming
frothy white foam
and bubbles of breath
fortuitous dream-laden domes to caress.

the Geography of Light!

Mountainous valleys and deserts of sand
prosperous plains and jungles of land
shadows of growth
oblique greening leaves
shelter the undergrowth of humus and seeds
night-vails of rest prowl with life's other side
giving strength   and moonlit timeless tides
yet
sadly, we've prodded and plundered the earth
molding cities of cement
whose crusted facades I lament
grow nothing but money on nebulous land

How fearfully our human hands shape the basis on which we stand
under the Light from the heavens above
changing the face of the Earth and its acceptance of Love
Human hands are the geography of Change
casting Light and Shadow across the Range
of the cultures we've plundered
or irreverently cast asunder.

As our Perspective
Creates the topography of

Dominance and War
whose
artificial light overshadows objects of worth
creating distorted visions of death and of birth
the night sky obscured
needs refreshing to view
in-depth and insight our constellations anew.
I'd hoped for a map
I often have asked
to give me insight

"Are there no Cartographers of the Geography of Light?

Everything's confusing and blurring my sight.
The Sun has eclipsed
the Earth holds her breath
folding in Faith it's blockbuster buildings

its highways and byways
running wires of heatwaves
as the trees give way
and the heavens lay waste.

Until

Finally
Quarantined in the Quiet

I Grow Leaves

and layers of bark

I Become the Tree.

my limbs stretching upwards and onwards soaking up Sun
   roots delving down deep dwelling in Dark
I'm leafing with stomas breathing with scope
Light receiving
        Life redeeming
   full throated Bird Song
         beseeching
this new Geography of Hope.

...the Geography of Light!

Hollywood Juniper

the Hollywood Juniper
has a propensity

for

striking a pose.

but it is never
more beautiful
than when the wind
has gnarled its branches
and twisted its trunk
into unabashed rapture.

***

i am the rules of the house
bent into shape
out of shape
written upon the walls in colors
you did not intend.

i am the language and the culture you taught me
punctuated
with words
that grew wings and found flight
in Webster's unabridged
dictionary.

i am long skirts
and long hair
modest in the face of fashion's revolving ruse.
yet ostentatious enough to elicit religion's sideways stare.

i am the well with its
dark waters
and blind fish.

i am the wind in the treetops
    blowing without a trace.
i am the depths of hell
    raised up by grace.

i am the silence in the storm
i am   the other cheek
            the second mile
the secret song
the smiles   the tears   the questionings   all along.

i am daringly dyslexic
no longer apologetic.

i am the values you taught me
    taken a turn
        you did not expect.

i am too sensitive hypothalamus
    unregulated neurotransmitters
i am cortex
i am the hormonal sex.

i am deep depression
    high elation
i am all of my/your creation

i am the seed you planted, watered and fed
i am the child you led

i am blown in the wind
    mangled in the storm
i am environmentally changed, completely rearranged.

i am alive from within.

i am Hollywood Juniper.

I am a Hollow Tree

now I understand.

I am alive surrounding
this wound
    this gaping wound exposing my heart

   It has Hollowed me

it has eaten away
what was dead: the heartwood of my past lay dormant
  no longer protected
      it decayed and released rich nutrients into the xylem
of my existence
    my whole core emptied and flowed into living tissue
budding leaves reaching green for the Sun

transforming Light into Life
    I grow

Hollowed
  yet thriving
 the sapwood of my life surrounds, houses and protects a
                host of diversity:
Bluebirds, raccoons, flying squirrels, albino squirrels,
woodpeckers, owls, and wrens,
chickadees, bees, bats, and mice,
   the prickly porcupine!

we will all thrive together.

There is no other way.

What a rare and beautiful
existence.

Hollowed
I am Hallowed.

I was fascinated as I read about hollow trees. I learned that a **dead tree canNot** become hollow...only a LIVING tree. It does not kill the tree. I love the concept that the interior wood is dead already (it is full of resins and toxins so it can no longer transport water and nutrients to the tree) and is not useful anymore except structurally ... a hollow tree has the advantage structurally of bending with the wind and not breaking. The wound exposes the dead wood so micro-organisms and fungi can break down the nutrients stored there (not accessible otherwise) and the Tree can then feed on those nutrients that it could not use before. The Hollow is also the only way a tree can take a diverse array of animals into its very heart... because it is empty of all that is dead that it could not use. Squirrels and birds can live in a tree's branches...BUT that is not the same as the protection from the environment of living inside the heart of a Living Hollow Tree! It takes a Wound, an Injury! for this to happen.

How beautifully life manifests itself imbued with meaning.

This is the reality of our own lives too! If we are going to be able to take others who are VASTLY different than we are into our **Heart**, we have to have a space for them! We have to be emptied of all that is dead and useless in our heart and be fed by the humus of it first. Trees can house animals in their branches...we can hold people at "arms-length" and think we are doing all we can...but that is kind of like mere "tolerance" in my mind...to actually embrace them as ourself...to take someone vastly different INTO our hearts...we have to be like a hollow tree...

I understand better now about the wounds of my life. I do not want to keep the hollow in my heart empty...I want to fill it... housing any and all who need embracing and a "home". This, to me, is the Love of G0d.

Burls!

Points of Reference

Every Point-of-View
  is a view-from-a-Point
    no matter how High and Mighty
the Straight grained
   Trunk
     reaches Up
 it grows around its straight grained truth.
But, my wounded wood
  my viral infected trunk
bleeds bulging tumors
that sprout. twist. turn.
  compress and congregate every single Point into

a cathedral of bark-domed Galls.

 Burls

bursting with a
  Million Points of Unborn buds
      churning in Tree-Time:
 a Fractal of immense
      imagination
  engrained in delirious xylem
transporting living water with swirling
   artistry...patterned into a million Points of Reference

Until i am felled by the forces of the Earth

Then. my Burls.
   my Wounds
    born again from mangled encrusted heartwood
send down roots
    feed on the humus of straight grained decay
 sprout tender new leaves
   and
    reach for the Light.

Winter's Warp

Today
in Winter's Warp
Twisted among the barren branches
Whose porous bark is bedecked with lenticels not leaves
No stomas
for quick and easy exchange,
yet they Breathe.
So today in this cold atmosphere, a paradox of doubt, yet free from fear
I'll Breathe like the trees.
I too am clearly Devoid of leaves.
through the bleak winter wasteland
where Burrowed in earth
my tiny hair roots seek pockets of beetle breath
aerated once by wriggling worms
who silently danced in undulating mirth
furtively feasting filling belly and beauty for all they were worth.

Today
I walk among the trees
Their antient song:
the oxygen I breathe
a lighter way on earth I know
to tread in silence
and let them show
me how to live and learn and grow
with patience practiced day by day
and faith that here and now
through cold and snow
as their bare branches lace the clouds with fingers feathered
have given birth before the

Frozen Earth
blew her words into whitened skies

and crisp clear stars and a moon that glowed
proclaiming constantly
        there will be
in rounds of sunrise/sunset
            ephemeral colors
  slowly slowly eternal Mother
stir the ground with your seasonal glance
        downward inward outward upward
                        into your glorious greening stance.
Please.

A White Woman's Advice to herself:

Grow quietly like the trees
        they are both terrestrial
                        and celestial.

All things die
    even the carrion beetles who
                consume the Earth
        into rebirth.

But the trees
            draw in
    The History   ground down
        suck it in
            and Fruit it back
                sweeter than we knew.

The trees are at home in the Earth
            they are Welcome in the Sky
  they dig their toes

        to China

while the trees in China
    delve deep
            and reach
their Roots up to Me.

Trees in South Carolina sport wigs of
        Spanish Moss
            ethereal epiphytes
                dancing in their hair.

All trees
        reach leafy fingers
                        into the air
  though some are spiny prickly
            things

while others heart-shaped
Angel's wings.

i wonder
Is the Sky round?
a blanket
or an illusion?
Do the clouds keep me from hearing the Sounds
of the Universe?

i must ask the Trees
they grow quietly and listen.

i sigh

My feet can't plant
their toes and grow to

China.

My head can't sport epiphytes
or gaze amongst the clouds

But,
when i grow quietly
like the trees
and listen
both China and the Stars
Welcome me.

A Poet's Hymn

One day a tree grew   until
the axe drew
blood
and the tree became pulp
became paper
became poem
became crane
and flew away.

This flat life
thin as paper
wings words
a poet's hymn
and when folded fast
by fertile hands:
a frog
an owl
a crane

to fly away on bended wing
to seek   at   Least
10,000 words of peace
no voice
will utter   save on soaring wing
a silent prayer
a wish to sing.

And so transformed
i fly
this once flat life
has died
in peace
as she who wings her words
a feast
and folds her hands
and then   became
a sign of hope:
an origami crane.

In Memory of the Trees

i stand in awe
of nimble fingers
folding fast

one flat sheet of paper:

"the fine Art of Paper Folding"

transforming my life into
an origami crane
to fly away between the
lines of time
on wings of hope
thin as paper

held against the morning light's sanguinary glow

the tangerine sun
born on the ashes
of the past:
the howling wildfires
and flaming forests, like

my own strange colored
life consumed
in destructive beauty.

now i glow in the ash of the
tangerine sun

and the only memory of the trees
is in the
crane and the color of the sun.

and the only memory of the trees
is in the
crane and the color of the sun.

Rome, Rosaries, and Religion

Emptied by the opulence of St. Peter's
i asked the Sky
"what is Holy?"
and she showed me the Stone Pines
towering high above the Vatican
and the Ruins
their feet firmly consecrated in the earth.

i asked the Stone Pines
"what is Holy?"
and they spoke through the wind
whose voice
gently shook the Pine Nuts to the Ground.

i asked the Ground "what is Holy?"
and it showed me
the Sparrow, the Pigeon and the Gull
eating crumbs

i asked the Gull "what is Holy?"
and she showed me the Pine Nut
lying on the cobblestones
chiseled centuries ago
by the labor of the lowly.

i asked the cobblestones "what is Holy?"
and they showed me the vender by the Tiber
roasting chestnuts with care
both his rosary and his prayer...

i asked the Tiber
"what is Holy?"
but the polluted waters
only sighed
until the rain began
to fill the Sky

the River
the Stone Pines
and my eyes.
So
i asked my eyes
"what is Holy?"

and the Stone Pines answered:

"Life is Holy."
and my breath understood.

Coppiced/Coped/Created

I have persevered through
Storms and strain
    Through Infestations and duress
  Gripped the Earth with the teeth of my roots
sucked up water and nutrients
    to mix with the Sun
       Light
          Power!
I have Talked through the Wind
    Sent out warnings to ward off disease
Signals of when
     To flower and speak to the bees.
I have Fruited to seed the land.

     until

I was coppiced
By the force
     of the Axe
In One
     Swift swing.
        Cut-to-the-quick.
Felled
  But not razed
     I Rise!
Sprout:
      Root Sprouts
         From My Vigorous
Underground Life
    Source
I suck up water and nutrients
  To Cope.
      I Surge upward from Every side
           into
        Light Opening vision.
           I Regenerate the Ancient Way…
                        to Uncover the Understory

Now Light eating plants can thrive
Tiny animals can hide.
I thrive along with them
we grow Up into the Light!

I have been struggling with "who I am" in old age. After losing Sheldon and all visage of our life. My body aged. I lost strength and balance … I felt cut down. Felled. Useless. I wondered if I'd ever be remotely able again. I asked myself: Do I want to live that way? No! So, I did NOT give up. Seeing trees that have been cut down suddenly spurred insight into my old, wrinkled body that had been knocked down flat and cut to the quick until every part I had recognized as "me" was gone. But i see now that although much of "me" is gone I can still be useful.

Coppiced/coped/created.
—Me. The body may be disabled but the Soul can still Fly.

This is Not a Poem

This is Not a poem
It is my Story
My Flesh.

It is the skin of my breath
Stretched taunt Through peace and through pain.
It is the rhythm
of soundwaves bathed in the ocean of Life
It is the sea turtle's
Plunge to the depths and the heights
As the wings in my cavernous chest
Take Flight.
It is my road in the Dark
With ominous trees speaking Truth in the Wind
It is the song in the morning
The sweet savor of the meadow lark's
Life.
It is the bruises i hid in turmoil and strife.

It is the Lilies like blood
at rest on the tomb
It is the dance of the glorious phases of the moon.

It is the grief of my childhood
spun through my pores
It is the tears of my
Mother lost in my arms
as my calloused hands knit patience to keep me warm.

It is the cradle of innocence in the depths of my soul
It is the story i tell myself to keep myself whole.

It is the tears and the fears
The joys and the peace
It is my life wound round
my orchestrated sound.

It is the song in my heart as nearing the end
i listen with gratefulness
To the story life sends
Written anew
my words create wisdom
to see
through the portholes of Time

the dynamics of Life's Panoramic Paradigm.

This is not a poem.

This is the pain of my birth in the womb of the World.
This is my thirst in the desert, the barren laid waste
The peaks and the pinnacles
that strengthened my limbs
The sunlight transformed through thick and
through thin.
This is my flowering seeds stretching up to meet
Heaven's Rim.

This is my Ripe Fruit grown
Wild beneath my skin.

This is Not a Poem

This is my Story.

My Flesh.

Martha Sherick Shen is native to Iowa. Born into an academic family, she was labeled a slow learner years before dyslexia was understood. She did not read until she was 13 years old. Suddenly, reading became her world of wonder and writing became her expression. It was a private blossoming, however, since it did not change the way people saw her. After raising her daughters and divorcing, she earned a degree in Zoology from Iowa State University within a specialized program for Neuroscience and Physiological Psychology. She graduated with honors in 2003. During these years, Martha also met, befriended, and later married the man who would bring her a fairytale life, Sheldon Shen. She has written poetry privately throughout her life. Martha's first published poem resides with *Flying Island Literary Journal.* Her second published poem won BEST of *Synkroniciti*'s Summer 2024 issue and has been nominated for Best of the Net for 2023-2024. Martha also has poems published in Silver Birch Press' *ALL ABOUT MY MOTHER* Series and *FAVORITE THINGS* Series, and two poems in *Synkroniciti*'s "Identity" issue. She was a semi-finalist in Finishing Line Press' 2025 Open Chapbook Competition with this, her first chapbook, *Waning into Winter.* Martha lives in Des Moines, Iowa with her daughter Abra's family and her French Bulldog, Judah.

www.ingramcontent.com/pod-product-compliance
Lightning Source LLC
LaVergne TN
LVHW090540110826
845146LV00003B/1192

* 9 7 9 8 8 9 9 9 0 3 9 8 4 *